A Community Cares and Shares

Diana Noonan

A Community Cares and Shares

Text: Diana Noonan
Series consultant: Annette Smith
Publishing editor: Simone Calderwood
Editor: Amy Nicholls-Diver
Project editor: Annabel Smith
Designers: James Lowe and Karen Mayo
Series designers: James Lowe and Karen Mayo
Photo researcher: Debbie Gallagher
Production controller: Erin Dowling
Reprint: Siew Han Ong

PM Guided Reading
Emerald Level 25

ISBN 978 0 17 036898 8

Cengage Learning Australia
Level 5 , 80 Dorcas Street
Southbank VIC 3006
Phone: 1300 790 853
Email: aust.nelsonprimary@cengage.com

For learning solutions, visit cengage.com.au

Acknowledgements
We would like to thank the following for permission to reproduce copyright material:

Front cover, pp. 1, 4: iStockphoto/Susan Chiang; pp. 3, 10 (left): iStockphoto/Steve Debenport; p. 5 (top): Shutterstock.com/Hurst Photo, (bottom): Newspix/Robert Pozo; p. 6 (top): Shutterstock.com/Monkey Business Images, (bottom): iStockphoto/Pamela Moore; p. 7: Lindsay Edwards/Cengage Learning Australia; p. 8: Shutterstock.com/wavebreakmedia; p. 9: Getty Images/Kinzie+Riehm; p. 10 (right): Lindsay Edwards/Cengage Learning Australia; p. 11: iStockphoto/Susan Chiang; p. 12: Newspix/Stephen Cooper; p. 13: Getty Images/Cyrus McCrimmon/The Denver Post; p. 15: Newspix/Braden Fastier; p. 16, back cover: Getty Images/Nadya Lukic; p. 17: Shutterstock.com/Monkey Business Images; pp. 18–19: Alamy/Visuals Stock; p. 20: Fairfax Syndication/SMH/Brendan Esposito; p. 21: Fairfax Syndication/The Sun Herald; pp. 22–23: Fairfax Syndication/The Age/Rodger Cummins; p. 24: Shutterstock.com/Syda Productions; p. 25: Alamy/Alex Segre; p. 26: Shutterstock.com/Monkey Business Images; p. 27 (top): iStockphoto/Susan Chiang, (bottom): Getty Images/Siri Stafford; p. 28: Getty Images/Thomas Barwick; p. 29: Fairfax Syndication/SMH/Wolter Peeters; p. 30: Getty Images/Joshua Hodge Photography; Design images pp. 24–30: Fairfax Syndication/SMH/Wolter Peeters (top), iStockphoto/Susan Chiang (bottom).

Every effort has been made to trace and acknowledge copyright. However, if any infringement has occurred, the publishers tender their apologies and invite the copyright holders to contact them.

Printed in China by 1010 Printing International Ltd
13 25

This product is made from materials that are compliant with the EU Deforestation Regulation

Contents

What Is a Community?

A community can be a group of people who live in the same area and look after each other. Or, it can be a group of people who share the same interests and **beliefs**, or who come from the same **culture**. People who live in communities often take good care of their **environment** and have fun together. They listen to each other's opinions and ideas, and help to make rules.

People work together in a community garden.

An older child teaches other children about recycling.

Children celebrate at a community festival.

Think and Talk About …

People can use the internet to find community groups in their local area.

A Community Cares for Its People

Most large communities have people who are paid to do their work, such as doctors, police officers, firefighters and teachers.

But many communities also have **volunteers** to help care for others.

Doctors are an important part of a community.

Children volunteer to help people in need.

Volunteers sometimes include school students who can help in different ways. One way school students can care for others in their community is by volunteering at a local kindergarten. The students and their teacher can make short visits to the kindergarten three or four times a year, to help the younger children get ready for starting school.

An older child talks to a younger child about starting school.

Think and Talk About ...

Some adults volunteer at schools. They might help students with their reading or assist on excursions.

A student reads to younger children.

The students can help by reading to the younger children or playing with them. Sometimes, they may be asked to set out equipment for an activity. When a kindergarten child is ready to start school, a volunteer student may be asked to show them around the classrooms and playground. They may also become the younger child's buddy for a few weeks. This helps the younger child feel safe and happy about starting school.

Everyone has a safe and enjoyable time when volunteers know the kindergarten's rules. School students can find out what these rules are by talking to their own teachers before they visit.

Most kindergartens share some of the same rules. These may include: do not bring your own food into the kindergarten; always close the security gates behind you; never take children for a walk outside the kindergarten unless a teacher is with you; speak softly; make sure children wash their hands before eating; get help from a teacher if a child is upset.

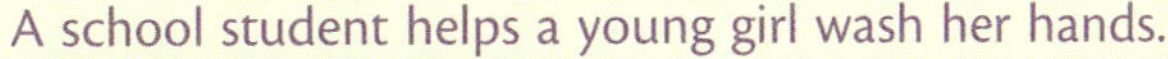

A school student helps a young girl wash her hands.

Student volunteers can also help their local kindergarten by donating items. Some students make books, which they give to the kindergarten to use in their library. Others collect and clean items that the kindergarten children use in games and activities. These include recycled plastic bottles, and pieces of wood and fabric.

It is important to first ask the kindergarten teachers what items would be useful. Volunteers should find out about any items that are not wanted because they could be dangerous for small children.

When people grow out of their clothes, they can be given to others.

Kindergarten children can use plastic bottles in many art and craft activities.

Think and Talk About ...

Some student volunteers help out at animal shelters. They can exercise the animals and keep them entertained.

Animals in shelters need lots of attention and care.

By visiting a kindergarten or other local group, student volunteers lend a helping hand and find out more about their own community and how it works.

A Community Cares for Its Environment

Special workers are **employed** by most large communities to look after the environment. Some workers collect waste and recycled materials. They take **green waste** to composting sites. Road sweepers drive trucks that brush the streets clean. Water officers make sure no **pollution** enters lakes and streams.

Workers collect household rubbish in a large truck.

Food-safety officers check cafés to make sure food is safe for the customers to eat. Without these and many other workers, a community's environment would not be as clean and safe as it is.

But community workers do not have time to look after every part of the local environment, and that is where volunteers can help out. Community volunteers work together to clean up special areas of their environment, such as walking trails and beaches.

A food safety worker inspects a café.

Many communities **rely** on volunteers to help with an **annual** clean-up at a beach, park or nature reserve. It is important to make sure that rubbish from every part of the environment is removed and that all the volunteers stay safe as they work.

On the day of the clean-up, all the volunteers meet. The person in charge organises the volunteers into teams. Each team decides who the leader will be. The teams listen carefully to the clean-up rules. These include:

- wear gloves to protect hands from cuts and dirt
- use tongs to pick up sharp objects
- sort rubbish into different piles for recycling
- wear a sun hat and sunscreen
- stay within hearing distance of the team leader.

Think and Talk About ...

On Clean Up Australia Day, thousands of people all around the country clean up their local environment.

The volunteers agree that if they find any rubbish they think may be dangerous, they will leave it where it is and tell their team leader. The team leader will decide what to do with that piece of rubbish. Each team is given an area to clean up. When all the rubbish has been collected, most of it is taken to a waste and recycling centre.

Volunteers work together to clean an area of bushland.

Community clean-up days are important, and not just because they keep the environment clean. As the volunteers work together, they learn more about the other people who live in their community. Volunteers find out about others' ideas, opinions and culture, and may even find themselves working alongside neighbours they have never met!

Children get to know each other through volunteering together.

It is important that children learn about recycling.

Think and Talk About …

Some volunteer organisations come to schools to teach students about recycling.

A Community Has Fun Together

Everyone in a community helps to make sure that the area they live in is a safe and enjoyable place. They can do this by taking turns at being community leaders and deciding on community rules. They also fundraise for important projects. Being part of a community can be hard work, so every now and then, everyone needs to celebrate all the good things that have been done. Communities do this by making a time and place for everyone to have fun together.

People laugh and play with coloured powders during Holi, a Hindu festival in India.

Think and Talk About ...

Communities around the world celebrate together in many different ways. People might dress up in costumes, eat special foods or exchange gifts during these celebrations.

Many communities have fun together by holding a festival. A festival often has a **theme**. For example, a community group that is well known for growing a certain vegetable, or making a certain type of food, might hold a food festival.

People buy dim sum at a food festival.

Children wear traditional Greek costumes at a Greek community festival.

At festivals, people from similar backgrounds might take part in a street parade, where they dress up in traditional clothing. People might cook food using their own special recipes, and sell the food at street stalls. People might perform traditional dances at this festival.

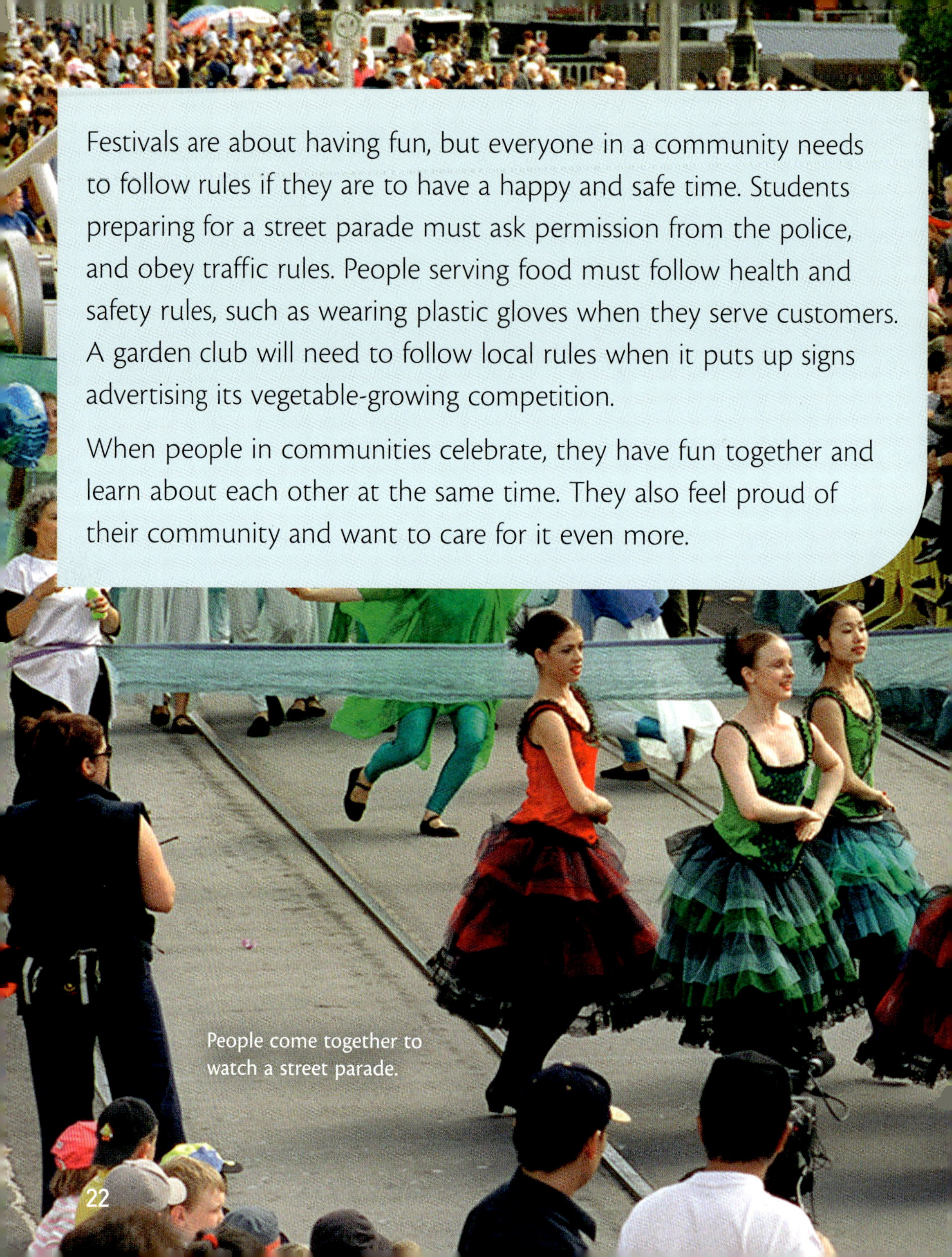

Festivals are about having fun, but everyone in a community needs to follow rules if they are to have a happy and safe time. Students preparing for a street parade must ask permission from the police, and obey traffic rules. People serving food must follow health and safety rules, such as wearing plastic gloves when they serve customers. A garden club will need to follow local rules when it puts up signs advertising its vegetable-growing competition.

When people in communities celebrate, they have fun together and learn about each other at the same time. They also feel proud of their community and want to care for it even more.

People come together to watch a street parade.

RSEA
RSEA
event staff

No Outdoor Gym in Our Park!

To: Henley District Council

From: Year 5A,
Henley School

Subject: Henley East Park

Dear Councillors

We have been told that the council wants to build an outdoor gym in the Henley East park. The council says an outdoor gym will help everyone in our community become fitter.

We use the playground in the park a lot, and we don't agree with the council's plans. First, we think there are already enough ways for the people in our community to become fit. Second, we believe that an outdoor gym will bring too many adults near to the playground. They will be doing fast exercises and will make the park crowded. This might make us feel unsafe, because it will be harder to run around and play games. And finally, we think that the council could spend the money to make the playground equipment better.

A gym in our park will bring more adults near to where we play.

We believe that the people in our community already have enough ways to get fit. Adults can go to the indoor gyms. Also, adults and children have sports grounds, cycle and walking tracks, and swimming pools. Children have playgrounds to help them keep fit.

Henley East park has an amazing climbing wall, a fun adventure course and an exciting skateboard area. We have a wide, grassy field where we run around and play tag and ball games. An outdoor gym would take up most of the field. This would make us less fit, not more!

The council says that the park will become a place for everyone, not just children and their parents. If there is an outdoor gym, many more adults will come to the park to exercise. Children may not feel comfortable playing if there are grown-ups exercising in the same place. We don't think we will have space to play safely with lots of adults near to the playground. Children like running around and playing games. This will be harder if there are grown-ups exercising where we are playing.

We believe that if the council has money to spend on the Henley East park, it should be used to buy more equipment for the playground. It could also be used to fix some of the equipment as it gets old and broken. We would also like to see a goal net built at one end of the field, so we can play soccer.

We would like the council to make improvements to our playground.

We know that the council wants to do its best for our community, but we don't want an outdoor gym near to our playground. We think playgrounds are for playing. We want them to be special places that are just for children.

Thank you for taking the time to read our email.

Year 5A children,
Henley School

Glossary

annual (*adjective*)	happening once a year
beliefs (*noun*)	strong feelings that something exists or is true
culture (*noun*)	a group's ideas and background
employed (*verb*)	paid to do work
environment (*noun*)	the natural world
green waste (*noun*)	waste that was once growing, such as grass cuttings or branches from a tree
pollution (*noun*)	something that is harmful to the environment
rely (*verb*)	to need or depend on something
theme (*noun*)	a very important idea
volunteers (*noun*)	people who help or do work somewhere but are not paid

Index